UNDERSTANDING RHETORIC

A Graphic Guide to WRITING

Elizabeth Losh
Jonathan Alexander
Kevin Cannon
Zander Cannon

BEDFORD / ST. MARTIN'S

BOSTON • NEW YORK

For Bedford/St. Martin's

Senior Executive Editor: Leasa Burton
Executive Editor: Carolyn Lengel
Senior Production Editor: Deborah Baker
Senior Production Supervisor: Jennifer Peterson
Executive Marketing Manager: Molly Parke
Editorial Assistants: Daniel Schafer, Leah Rang
Copy Editor: Arthur Johnson
Indexer: Mary White
Permissions Manager: Kalina K. Ingham
Senior Art Director: Anna Palchik
Cover Illustrators: Kevin Cannon, Zander Cannon
Printing and Binding: RR Donnelley and Sons

President, Bedford/St. Martin's: Denise B. Wydra
Presidents, Macmillan Higher Education: Joan E. Feinberg and Tom Scotty
Editor in Chief: Karen S. Henry
Director of Development: Erica T. Appel
Director of Marketing: Karen R. Soeltz
Production Director: Susan W. Brown
Associate Production Director: Elise S. Kaiser
Managing Editor: Elizabeth Schaaf

Manufactured in the United States of America.

8 7 6 5 4 3
f e d c b

For information, write: Bedford/St. Martin's, 75 Arlington Street, Boston, MA 02116
   (617-399-4000)

ISBN 978-0-312-64096-5

Acknowledgments

Acknowledgments and copyrights appear at the back of the book on page 277, which constitutes an extension of the copyright page. It is a violation of the law to reproduce these selections by any means whatsoever without the written permission of the copyright holder.

CONTENTS

Contents

PREFACE:
GETTING GRAPHIC

Understanding Rhetoric is the work of many hands and many years—a project that attempts to combine some of the best knowledge and practices from the teaching of writing with a forward-thinking approach to visual and multimodal literacy.

You'll find that this book covers all the commonly taught topics in first-year composition, offering time-tested techniques for improving critical analysis, argumentation, and the development of research questions in college writing. It contains practical tips for improving organization, identifying bias, evaluating sources, representing scholarly debates, and avoiding plagiarism.

It also reflects the latest research in composition, which focuses on the development of writers as well as writing.

In short, this is an effective classroom text that is thoroughly grounded in scholarship.

But perhaps the most unusual feature of this book—the one that you can't help noticing—is that this is a comic book. When we began to work on this book, we hoped that by emphasizing multimodal approaches to composing, we would engage student writers in thinking about their identities, contexts for their research, and effective writing processes. But we also wanted to create a book that students would actually want to read—a book that could make rhetoric interesting and maybe even enjoyable.

"ENGAGING AND LIGHTHEARTED, BUT ALSO CAREFULLY ORGANIZED, THEORETICALLY SOUND, AND A COMPELLING WAY TO TEACH STUDENTS ABOUT CRITICAL READING AND WRITING IN A TECHNOLOGICALLY ADVANCED, INFORMATION-RICH SOCIETY."

Michael Pemberton,
Georgia Southern University

Increasingly, composition instructors recognize that students need a range of literacy skills. The Web, video, blogging, YouTube, Tumblr, and social network sites complement and challenge traditional text-based literacy practices, and students must consider the rhetorical requirements of writing for multimodal platforms and also think about graphic design and visual evidence as part of their basic tools for communication. After all, many of them may be doing most of their writing using such platforms.

Many writing instructors have begun using comics in the composition classroom to engage students with writing that is both textually and visually rich. The visual dimension of the text doesn't simply illustrate rhetorical concepts; rather, the images and text must be read in tandem for the reader to fully grasp the concepts being discussed. In composing *Understanding Rhetoric*, we decided to capitalize on such pedagogical energy by talking about rhetoric in the medium of a graphic book.

Understanding Rhetoric is arranged into eight "issues" dealing with particular rhetorical concepts, each using a different accent color.

- Every issue begins with a chapter featuring somewhat hyperbolic versions of "Liz and Jonathan," who interact with historical and comic-book characters (and with illustrators and coauthors Kevin Cannon and Zander Cannon). Most chapters include a quick-reference chart recapping important ideas.
- A "ReFrame" section after each chapter features two student characters, Luis and Cindy, grappling with that chapter's concepts and "walking through" one of a variety of texts.
- A "Drawing Conclusions" spread at the end of each issue suggests assignments that will allow students to try the concepts out for themselves.

"A HIP, CONTEMPORARY, AND WITTY EXPLANATION OF THE HISTORY AND SIGNIFICANCE OF RHETORIC FOR THE DIGITAL AGE."

Adam Bessie,
Diablo Valley College

"THIS TEXT IS FUN. IT MAKES PEOPLE WANT TO COME BACK TO THE IDEAS AGAIN AND AGAIN."

Chris Gerben,
Stanford University

As you read through the text with your classes, ask students to pay attention not only to what the characters are saying, but to how information about writing and composing is conveyed both textually and visually. Our hands-on style emphasizes an active approach to writing, reading, and responding to all kinds of texts and emphasizes the dialogic nature of successful academic and public writing.

Ultimately, to enter into conversations (in good Burkean fashion) in different public spheres, writers should work through a series of interactions and discussions that allow them to craft insightful positions and compelling arguments. Our characters show how all writing is connected to identities. People write from particular positions, stances, and senses of self, and having a greater awareness of those positions—social, cultural, political, and historical—makes for more sophisticated and assured composing.

We hope you and your students enjoy *Understanding Rhetoric*. We also invite you to check out the instructor's manual and Student Site for further samples and teaching ideas, along with information about how our book supports the Council of Writing Program Administrators (WPA) Outcomes, at **bedfordstmartins.com/understandingrhetoric**.

Most importantly, feel free as you teach with this book to talk back to us. Dare to disagree, either with us or other characters in the book. Get graphic with the text, and invite your students to draw and write within it. You might find yourself working with your students to make your own graphic guide to writing!

"I AM VERY EAGER TO TEACH USING THIS BOOK."

Ginger Jurecka Blake,
University of Wisconsin

AUTHOR ACKNOWLEDGMENTS

We appreciate the contributions of the many, many individuals whose expertise and advice made this book possible.

Reviewers

We received invaluable feedback from a wonderful group of reviewers, whose suggestions helped us shape the direction of individual chapters and of the book as a whole during its entire development process: Tom Amorose, Seattle Pacific University; Max Badesheim III, Boise State University; Kim Ballard, Western Michigan University; Joseph Bartolotta, University of Minnesota; Diane Forbes Berthoud, University of California, San Diego; Adam Bessie, Diablo Valley College; Ginger Jurecka Blake, University of Wisconsin; Lady Branham, University of Oklahoma; Beth Buyserie, Washington State University; James "Bucky" Carter, University of Texas at El Paso; Christine Cucciarre, University of Delaware; Kathryn E. Dobson, McDaniel College; Sergio C. Figueiredo, Clemson University; John Garrison, University of California, Davis; Oriana Gatta, Georgia State University; Chris Gerben, Stanford University; Mathew Gomes, California State University, Fresno; Jim Haendiges, Dixie State College of Utah; Levia Hayes, College of Southern Nevada; Fred Johnson, Whitworth University; Jeraldine Kraver, University of Northern Colorado; Nate Kreuter, Western Carolina University; Bradley Lane, North Seattle Community College; Matthew Levy, Pacific Lutheran University; Kelli Moore, University of California, San Diego; Shannon R. Mortimore-Smith, Shippensburg

University; Michael Pemberton, Georgia Southern University; Erin Presley, University of Georgia; Scott Reed, University of Georgia; Molly Scanlon, Virginia Tech; Cheri Lemieux Spiegel, Northern Virginia Community College; Michael Sutcliffe, Washington State University Vancouver; Phil Troutman, George Washington University; Christopher Werry, San Diego State University; Alan Williams, Illinois State University; and Joseph Willis, Southern Utah University.

Contributors
We would like to acknowledge those whose ideas and publications helped in the creation of this book: Norah Ashe, University of Southern California; Greg Benford, University of California, Irvine; Vinayak Chaturvedi, University of California, Irvine; Michael Clark, University of California, Irvine; James Paul Gee, Arizona State University; Brook Haley, University of California, Irvine; Michael Householder, Southern Methodist University; Julia Lupton, University of California, Irvine; Steven Mailloux, Loyola Marymount University; Lynn Malley, University of California, Irvine; Michele Mason, University of Maryland; Robert Moeller, University of California, Irvine; Erika Nanes, University of Southern California; John Stauffer; Ellen Strenski; Brook Thomas, University of California, Irvine; Phil Troutman, George Washington University; and Ann Van Sant, University of California, Irvine.

For allowing us to adapt a paragraph from her student essay on Japanese Americans in internment camps during World War II, many thanks to Marissa Osato, a graduate of the University of California, Irvine.

For contributions to our thinking on the instructor's manual for *Understanding Rhetoric*, our gratitude goes to Henry Jenkins, Keith McCleary, Emily Roxworthy, Molly Scanlon, Cynthia Selfe, and Wayne Yang.

We thank Tom Gammill for his illustrations in Chapter 5.

We are grateful to Thomas LeBien of Hill & Wang and to Jessica Marshall of Eye Candy Books for helpful initial feedback on this project.

Finally, we would like to thank Zander Cannon and Kevin Cannon, our coauthors, for turning our manuscript into a real comic book. They contributed not just illustrations, but also many great ideas for conveying concepts visually—and a lot of good jokes.

Bedford/St. Martin's
Everyone on the team at Bedford/St. Martin's was critical for bringing this publication to fruition. Constructive and creative feedback—from Leasa Burton, Carolyn Lengel, Allie Goldstein, Daniel Schafer, Leah Rang, Karrin Varucene, Joan Feinberg, and Denise Wydra—over the course of many lively conversations was central to our writing process. We are grateful to Anna Palchik for her art direction; to our project editor, Deb Baker, and our copy editor, Arthur Johnson; to Karita dos Santos for market development; and to our marketing manager, Molly Parke.

Elizabeth Losh, *University of California, San Diego*
Jonathan Alexander, *University of California, Irvine*

We would like to thank everyone at Bedford/St. Martin's for their support, encouragement, and enthusiasm over the course of making this book. In particular we'd like to thank Leasa Burton and Carolyn Lengel for their vision and guidance in seeing this book through from an idea to a finished project, and we'd like to thank Anna Palchik and Deb Baker for their support on the art and technical end.

Big thanks also go out to our coauthors, Liz and Jonathan, for being nimble with their script and adaptable to the peculiarities of making a comic book, and to all the additional challenges of making that comic book informative and educational. Finally, we appreciate the support of Thomas LeBien, who recommended us as artists for *Understanding Rhetoric* in the first place.

Also, Zander would like to thank his wife Julie and their son Jin for their support and for making their home a happy place to return to at the end of the day.

Kevin Cannon
Zander Cannon

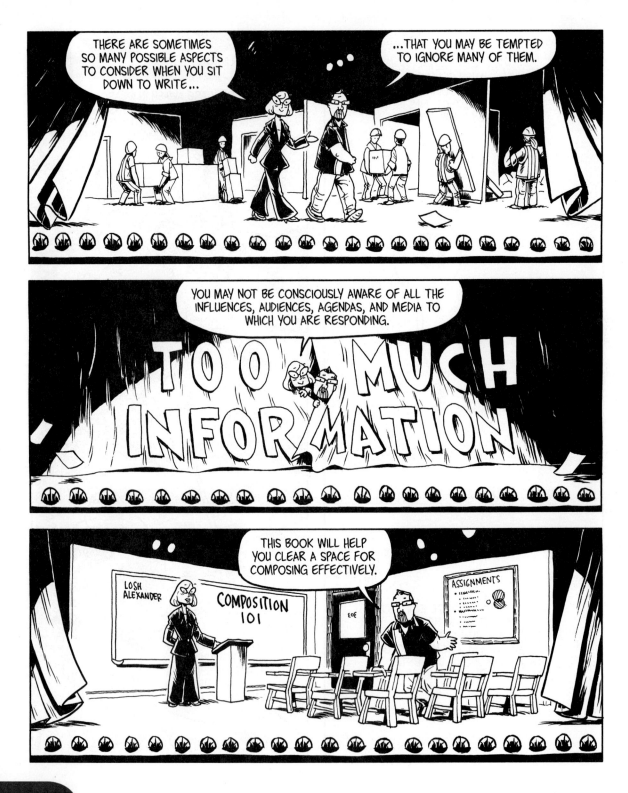

EXPLORING VISUAL LITERACY

CONSIDER THIS: WHEN A PHOTOGRAPH APPEARS IN THE PAGES OF A GRAPHIC NOVEL, WE KNOW THAT IT HAS A SPECIAL SIGNIFICANCE.

IT LOOKS DIFFERENT FROM THE OTHER PICTURES ON THE PAGE.

IT SEEMS TO DEPICT MORE ACCURATELY THE WAY THAT SOMEONE OR SOMETHING LOOKS IN REAL LIFE.

SO, AT THIS MOMENT, A PERSON WHO OPENS TO THESE PAGES IN THIS BOOK CAN COMPARE THE APPEARANCE OF THE CARTOON ME TO THE ME OF THE PHOTOGRAPH.

IT DOESN'T TAKE CAREFUL VIEWING TO SEE THAT THE ARTISTS HAVE SIMPLIFIED AND ABSTRACTED THE WAY JONATHAN LOOKS.

IN COMPARISON, THE PHOTOGRAPH PROBABLY SEEMS MUCH CLOSER TO SHOWING THE "REAL TRUTH."

WE USUALLY ASSOCIATE HAND-DRAWN IMAGES WITH WORKS OF THE IMAGINATION...

...WHILE PHOTOGRAPHS CREATED BY A MACHINE LIKE A CAMERA ARE SUPPOSED TO GIVE US THE REAL STORY, THE FACTS.

HOWEVER, WE KNOW THAT, JUST LIKE A DRAWING, A PHOTOGRAPH IS REALLY ONLY A REPRESENTATION.

DONK DONK

AFTER ALL, I CAN'T REACH IN AND ACTUALLY TOUCH THIS DESK.

MAYBE I CAN.

BUT THE READER CAN'T. IT'S A STATIC IMAGE THAT EXISTS ONLY IN TWO DIMENSIONS ON THE PAGE.

LEARNING TO READ THE DIFFERENT ELEMENTS OF A VISUAL TEXT IS PART OF WHAT WE CALL VISUAL LITERACY.

VISUAL LITERACY IS VERY IMPORTANT IN UNDERSTANDING THE MESSAGES THAT ARE CONVEYED BY PHOTOGRAPHY AND ILLUSTRATION...

...AND BY PAINTING, GRAPHIC DESIGN, SCULPTURE, ARCHITECTURE, VIDEO -- ANY MEDIA THAT WE ENGAGE WITH OUR EYES.

Introduction

DRAWING CONCLUSIONS

The following assignments ask you to try out the
concepts discussed in this introduction.

1 Think about your own writing
processes for various situations --
from formal (such as an academic
essay) to informal (such as
a comment on an online video).
Consider both individual work and
collaborations with others.

Map out what your processes look
like. What differences do you notice?
What prompts you to make changes
as you work through each process?

2 Watch a video of a person speaking to a live
or online audience (you might try TEDTalks to
find sources). Afterward, make notes on what
you remember most clearly; then watch the video
again, paying attention to what you see when the
most memorable information is presented.

What information does the speaker convey visually,
either with media accompanying the talk or with
body language? How well do the visuals and words
work together?

3 In the ReFrame for this chapter, Carol is working on her graphic memoir. Using both words and images, make a draft of what your own graphic memoir might look like.

What would you choose to emphasize? How would you make your central ideas and themes clear?

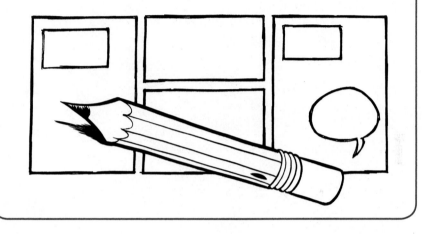

4 Comic artists often arrange panels to suggest different perceptions of time. Browse graphic novels or other comics to find creative depictions of the experience of passing time. Then create a storyboard for a short comic about an event that seemed to you to occur much more slowly or more quickly than you know it actually did.

Present your storyboard to others in your class and get feedback on how well your method works.

bedfordstmartins.com/understandingrhetoric

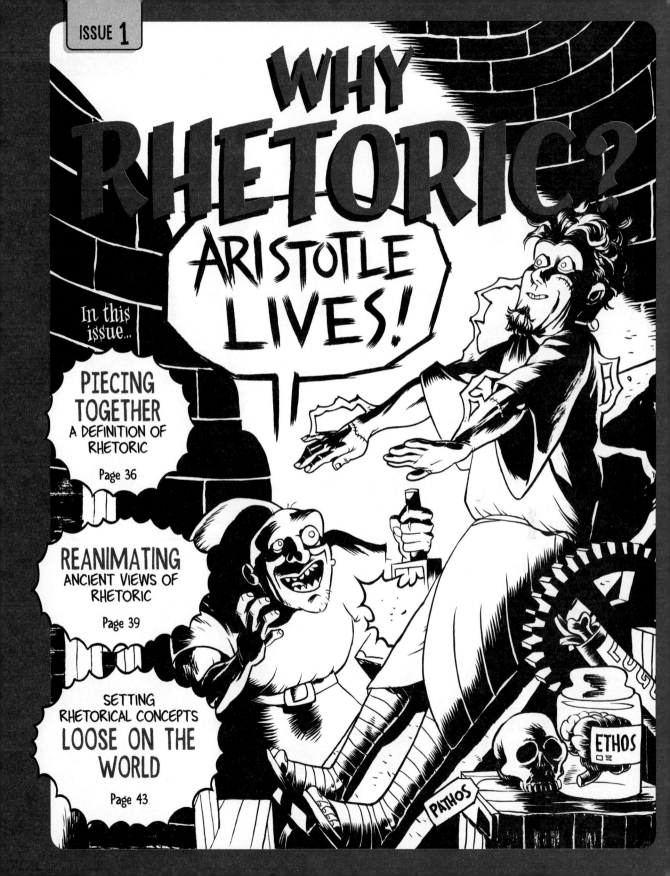

Issue 1 • Why Rhetoric?

REANIMATING ANCIENT VIEWS OF RHETORIC

MANY COMMONLY HELD NEGATIVE IDEAS ABOUT RHETORIC CAN BE TRACED TO THE ANCIENT GREEK PHILOSOPHER **PLATO**.

HE BELIEVED THAT TEACHERS LIKE US WHO TAUGHT RHETORIC WERE INSTRUCTING THEIR STUDENTS TO DECEIVE OTHERS RATHER THAN TO BETTER THEMSELVES.

IF SERIOUS DISCUSSION IS LIKE GYMNASTICS, THEN RHETORIC IS LIKE **COSMETICS**.

RHETORIC IS INTENDED ONLY TO HIDE FLAWS, NOT ENCOURAGE SELF-IMPROVEMENT.

PLATO (427–347 BCE)
ANCIENT GREEK PHILOSOPHER, STUDENT OF SOCRATES, AND FOUNDER OF THE ATHENIAN ACADEMY, AN IMPORTANT EARLY SCHOOL OF THOUGHT.

AS FAR AS PLATO WAS CONCERNED, RHETORIC WAS AN EMPTY, UNWHOLESOME DISTRACTION THAT TOOK ATTENTION AWAY FROM IMPORTANT PHILOSOPHICAL AND CIVIC MATTERS.

INDULGING THE POPULATION'S APPETITE FOR RHETORIC IS AS BAD AS SELLING **PASTRIES** INSTEAD OF DISPENSING **MEDICINE**.

PLATO ALSO THOUGHT THAT VIVID MEDIA EXPERIENCES, SUCH AS ANCIENT GREEK TRAGEDIES THAT SHOWED EXPLICIT SEX AND VIOLENCE, WOULD HAVE A BAD INFLUENCE ON YOUNG PEOPLE.

ALL POETS AND PLAYWRIGHTS SHOULD BE **BANISHED!**

ARISTOTLE WAS A PROPONENT OF THE USE OF RHETORIC TO PUT ACROSS A BROAD RANGE OF IDEAS.

ARISTOTLE (384–322 BCE)
ANCIENT GREEK PHILOSOPHER (AND STUDENT OF PLATO) WHOSE THINKING CONTRIBUTED MUCH TO THE DEVELOPMENT OF WESTERN EMPIRICAL AND SCIENTIFIC THOUGHT.

ARISTOTLE THOUGHT THAT PLAYS COULD SERVE AN **EDUCATIONAL** PURPOSE BY ENCOURAGING GREEK CITIZENS TO DEVELOP THEIR CAPACITIES FOR PITY AND FEAR.

BY SEEING THE CONSEQUENCES OF SEXUAL AND VIOLENT CRIMES THAT WERE COMMITTED BY ACTORS ON STAGE, SPECTATORS COULD LEARN **NOT** TO IMITATE **BAD ACTIONS.**

IN **THE ART OF RHETORIC,**

Aristotle has given us some powerful ways to think about Rhetoric and Communication:

ETHOS
PATHOS
LOGOS
KAIROS

ARISTOTLE SAYS THAT TO BE EFFECTIVE, A COMMUNICATOR HAS TO TAKE THREE CONCEPTS INTO CONSIDERATION:

ETHOS *ethical, ethics*

PATHOS *empathy*

LOGOS *logical*

STRANGE WORDS, BUT YOU CAN HEAR THEIR ENGLISH COUNTERPARTS QUITE CLEARLY...

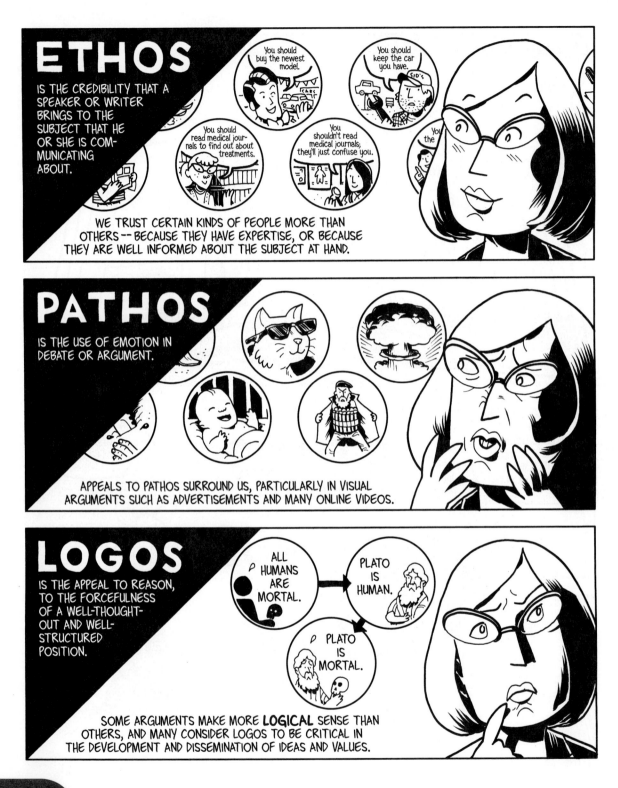

LEARNING TO RECOGNIZE THESE CONCEPTS WILL HELP YOU UNDERSTAND OTHER PEOPLE'S ARGUMENTS.

YOU'LL ALSO STRENGTHEN YOUR OWN POSITION AND THE WAY OTHERS SEE YOU.

ETHOS PATHOS LOGOS

ETHOS PATHOS LOGOS

FOR EXAMPLE, AN ONLINE PROFILE IS A RHETORICAL SPACE IN WHICH ETHOS, PATHOS, AND LOGOS ARE VERY IMPORTANT.

ONLINE PROFILES ALLOW USERS TO CREATE RICH, ENGAGING, AND SOMETIMES SATIRIC SELF-PORTRAITS.

Social Network

Jonathan is thinking about getting a new computer.

Plato: Pff! It would just be the shadow of the CONCEPT of a computer, anyway.

Aristotle: Ooh, but the new X432g's are so AWESOME!
1 DISLIKE

Jonathan wonders if he should eat some breakfast.

Aristotle: 1) Consider the pros and cons, 2) ask an expert, and 3) do it if you're hungry.

Jonathan likes:

Douglass Aristotle Jet-Skis

Lincoln Funny Hats The US Constitution

Asian Food Monkeys

THE MIX OF PICTURES, VIDEO, AND TEXT CAN ESTABLISH -- OR **DESTROY** -- YOUR CREDIBILITY, OR **ETHOS**.

FOR INSTANCE, IF JONATHAN, AS A PROFESSOR OF ENGLISH, HAS A PROFILE RIDDLED WITH TYPOS AND IMAGES OF HIM GETTING DRUNK WITH HIS STUDENTS...

Social Network

Jonathan: Oh HAI I am Drunk with studentz !!!1!!

HIS CREDIBILITY MIGHT **RISE** WITH SOME, BUT FALL WITH MOST OTHERS.

IMAGES AND WORDS CAN ALSO CONTRIBUTE TO THE PATHOS OF A PAGE...

ONE DAY:

Liz: is fine, keeping busy with work.

BUT THE NEXT:

Liz: is mourning the loss of a beloved cat.

"SNOOKUMS"
1999   2012

CERTAINLY, **PATHOS** IS BEING USED HERE TO PROMOTE SYMPATHY FOR LIZ...

...AND PERHAPS GENERATE A FEW KIND WORDS FOR HER **PAGE**.

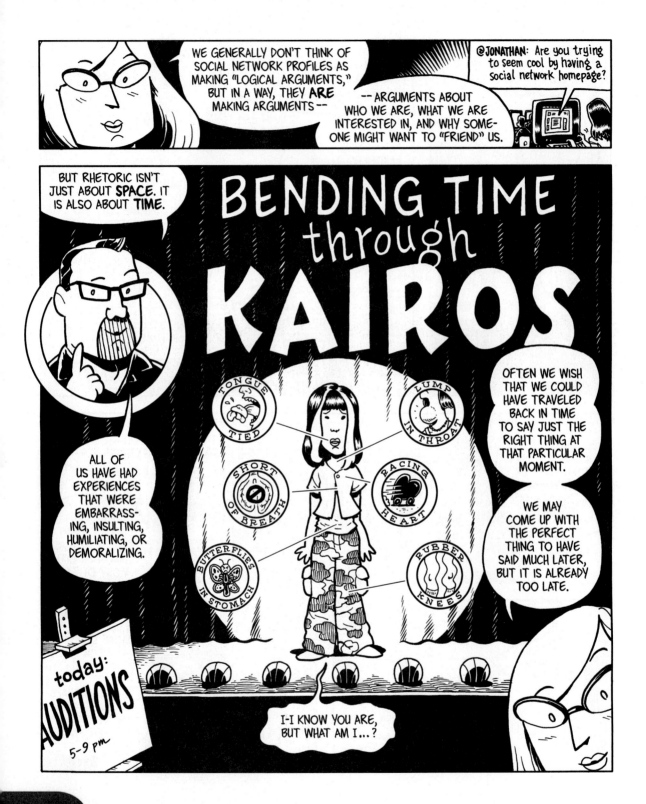

47

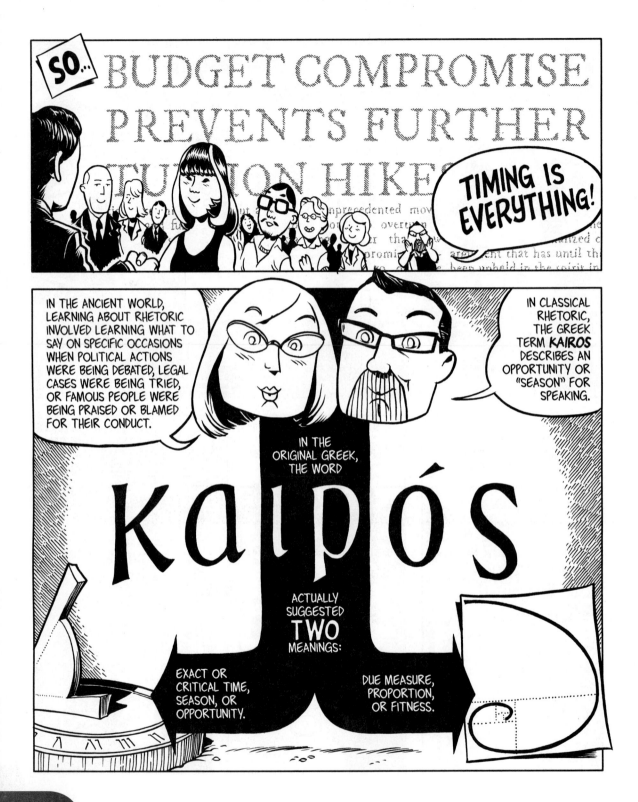

THE ROMAN RHETORICIAN **MARCUS TULLIUS CICERO** REALLY UNDERSTOOD THE IMPORTANCE OF KAIROS.

FOR EXAMPLE, WHEN HE WAS ABOUT TO BE EXECUTED ON ARBITRARY POLITICAL GROUNDS HE SAW A MOMENT FOR GRACIOUS WIT:

"There is nothing proper about what you are doing, soldier...

"...but at least make sure you cut off my head properly."

AFTER ALL, ARISTOTLE WASN'T THE **ONLY** FAMOUS RHETORICIAN IN THE ANCIENT WORLD.

CICERO, WHO LIKE MANY CULTURED ROMANS **ADMIRED** THE ANCIENT GREEKS, TRAINED ORATORS FOR THE ROMAN **SENATE**.

"No one can speak well, unless he thoroughly understands his subject."

CICERO (106–43 BCE)
ANCIENT ROMAN PHILOSOPHER, LAWYER, AND STATESMAN

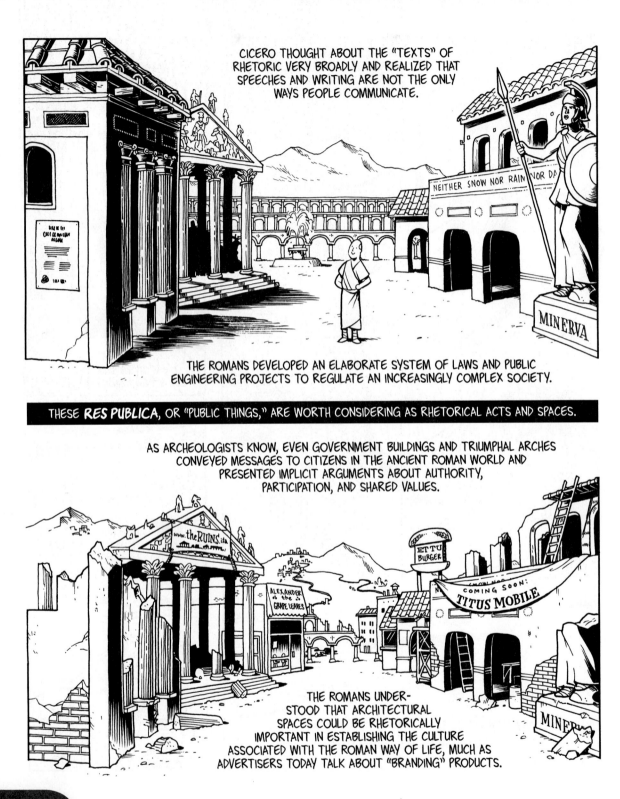

CICERO THOUGHT ABOUT THE "TEXTS" OF RHETORIC VERY BROADLY AND REALIZED THAT SPEECHES AND WRITING ARE NOT THE ONLY WAYS PEOPLE COMMUNICATE.

THE ROMANS DEVELOPED AN ELABORATE SYSTEM OF LAWS AND PUBLIC ENGINEERING PROJECTS TO REGULATE AN INCREASINGLY COMPLEX SOCIETY.

THESE **RES PUBLICA**, OR "PUBLIC THINGS," ARE WORTH CONSIDERING AS RHETORICAL ACTS AND SPACES.

AS ARCHEOLOGISTS KNOW, EVEN GOVERNMENT BUILDINGS AND TRIUMPHAL ARCHES CONVEYED MESSAGES TO CITIZENS IN THE ANCIENT ROMAN WORLD AND PRESENTED IMPLICIT ARGUMENTS ABOUT AUTHORITY, PARTICIPATION, AND SHARED VALUES.

THE ROMANS UNDERSTOOD THAT ARCHITECTURAL SPACES COULD BE RHETORICALLY IMPORTANT IN ESTABLISHING THE CULTURE ASSOCIATED WITH THE ROMAN WAY OF LIFE, MUCH AS ADVERTISERS TODAY TALK ABOUT "BRANDING" PRODUCTS.

TO:	l.losh@univ.edu
SUBJECT:	Upcoming Absence

Dear Dr. Losh,

My older brother is on active duty in the military and is being deployed this month. My extended family will have his going-away party on Friday. I'd very much like to be there, given the circumstances. May I be excused from class? I'll be happy to make up any work, and I will ask my classmates for notes.

Sincerely,

Luis

TO:	luis@univ.edu
SUBJECT:	RE: Upcoming Absence

Dear Luis,

Thanks for the heads-up. We'll be starting brainstorming and process work on your first assignment, an analysis of the design of a print advertisement for an on-campus organization, service, or cause.

You should analyze the rhetorical strategies of the advertisement by commenting on its logos, pathos, ethos, and kairos. You should study details in the wording, images, typography, organization, and visual design on the page. Let me know if you have any questions, and I'll see you in class on Monday.

Best,
Liz

DRAWING CONCLUSIONS

The following assignments ask you to practice thinking about the rhetorical strategies of **ETHOS**, **LOGOS**, **PATHOS**, and **KAIROS**.

1 Write an analysis of your social network page or the page of someone famous, such as a politician or celebrity. Make your analysis a *rhetorical* analysis by focusing on the use of logos, pathos, and ethos on the page.

Consider also the particular components of the Web page that allow a user to craft an identity online. What kinds of strategies help you and others compose with greater rhetorical effectiveness? Where and how on the page could its creator make more effective rhetorical choices?

2 Jot down some ideas about the rhetorical characteristics of informal and formal writing. In what ways are they similar? In what key ways are they different? Now, pick a kind of formal writing that you either are working on now or have encountered in the past.

Think about how a consideration of logos, ethos, pathos, and kairos could help you compose the piece better, or how it might have helped you improve a piece you've already written.

3

If you have a social network profile page, consider what you already know about the two meanings of kairos. What kinds of postings are intended to be appreciated during a period of only a day or even a few hours? What kinds of postings are intended to be seen for years to come?

Write an essay in which you describe your experience of kairos while using social network sites, and make some recommendations for your peers. Perhaps your essay can take the form of a "how to" guide.

4

This chapter incorporates many illustrations of ancient rhetoricians and philosophers. Find another image of Aristotle, Plato, or Cicero online -- perhaps from the ancient world or the Renaissance -- and compare it to the drawings in this book.

What do you think each image suggests about the person, and why do you think the image's creator wanted to give that impression?

bedfordstmartins.com/understandingrhetoric

"I have been frequently asked how I felt when I found myself in a free State. I have never been able to answer the question with any satisfaction to myself."

"It was a moment of the highest excitement I ever experienced."

"I suppose I felt as one may imagine the unarmed mariner to feel when he is rescued by a friendly man-of-war from the pursuit of a pirate."

WHAT'S THE DIFFERENCE IN EFFECT BETWEEN "HIGHEST EXCITEMENT" AND "GREATEST EXCITEMENT"?

I THINK "HIGHEST" IS A LOT MORE VIVID -- "HIGH" EVOKES AN ELEVATION IN STATUS, IN THIS CASE FROM SLAVE TO FREE CITIZEN.

"But the loneliness overcame me. There I was in the midst of thousands, and yet a perfect stranger; without home and without friends, in the midst of thousands of my own brethren—children of a common Father...

INTERESTING THAT HE SAYS "BRETHREN" AND "A COMMON **FATHER**" INSTEAD OF "BROTHERS AND SISTERS" OR "A COMMON **MOTHER**"?

IT COULD JUST BE A **GUY** THING.

...LET'S COME BACK TO THAT LATER.

"...and yet I dared not to unfold to any one of them my sad condition. I was afraid to speak to any one for fear of speaking to the wrong one...

"...and thereby falling into the hands of money-loving kidnappers, whose business it was to lie in wait for the panting fugitive...

"...as the ferocious beasts of the forest lie in wait for their prey."

AFTER ALL, ACCORDING TO **EYEWITNESSES**, THE REAL-LIFE DOUGLASS WAS ABOUT **SIX FEET TALL** AND VERY PHYSICALLY **IMPOSING**.

DOUGLASS WAS DEEPLY CONCERNED ABOUT THE WAY ILLUSTRATIONS IN BOOKS DEPICTED HIM.

BUT WE NEED TO DO SOME MORE **SYNTHESIS** TO PROVE THAT THESIS.

HERE'S A CLUE.

IN 1849 DOUGLASS PRAISED AN **ILLUSTRATED BOOK** ABOUT FAMOUS AFRICAN AMERICANS.

IN THE REVIEW, HE ALSO **RIDICULED** AN ILLUSTRATION OF HIMSELF, , WHICH HE SAID HAD A

"much more kindly and amiable expression, than is generally thought to characterize the face of a fugitive slave."

IN 1855 DOUGLASS CARE-FULLY CHOSE HIS PORTRAIT FOR THE NEWEST EDITION OF HIS BOOK, AN **ENGRAVING** FROM A **DAGUERREOTYPE** THAT HE HAD POSED FOR.

POOF

"I say, let him place himself in my situation—without home or friends—without money or credit—wanting shelter, and no one to give it—wanting bread, and no money to buy it,

"—and at the same time let him feel that he is pursued by merciless men-hunters..."

"—perfectly helpless both as to the means of defence and means of escape,

"—in the midst of plenty, yet suffering the terrible gnawings of hunger,—in the midst of houses, yet having no home,

"—among fellow-men, yet feeling as if in the midst of wild beasts, whose greediness to swallow up the trembling and half-famished fugitive is only equalled by that with which the monsters of the deep swallow up the helpless fish upon which they subsist,"

95

YOUR IDEAL READER FOR THE ESSAYS THAT YOU WRITE IN **COLLEGE** MAY BE VERY MUCH LIKE **YOURSELF**, PARTICULARLY IF YOU ARE PREPARING SOMETHING TO BE READ BY A GROUP OF **PEERS**.

OR YOUR IDEAL READER MIGHT BE MORE OF AN **EXPERT** ON THE SUBJECT TO WHOM YOU WILL WANT TO DEMONSTRATE YOUR **MASTERY** OF THE COURSE MATERIAL.

PEER

YOU

PROFESSOR

PUBLIC

IT IS ALWAYS HELPFUL TO ENVISION A READER **APPROPRIATE** TO A GIVEN PURPOSE AND TO THE PARTICULAR RHETORICAL OCCASION OR **KAIROS**.

YOU MAY THINK YOU DON'T KNOW ENOUGH ABOUT **FREDERICK DOUGLASS** OR THE **PRE-CIVIL WAR PERIOD** IN U.S. HISTORY TO UNDERSTAND WHAT DOUGLASS WANTED READERS TO KNOW.

BUT ANY READER WHO PAYS ATTENTION AND USES SMART READING STRATEGIES CAN LEARN TO EXPLICATE A TEXT AND UNCOVER MEANINGS.

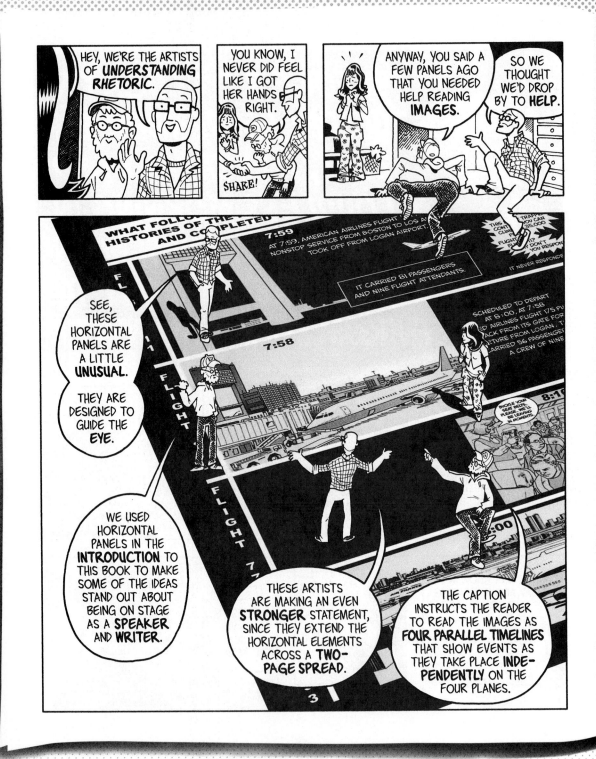

COMING UP IN THE NEXT EXCITING EPISODE OF **REFRAME**

"What's my IDENTITY?"

[pg. 135]

109

DRAWING CONCLUSIONS

The activities below ask you to focus on the rhetorical
dimensions of texts and visuals you might write about.

1 Choose one print text and one nonprint
text that you are currently reading.
Consider all of the ways you "notate"
what you read, either in writing or
in your head. Do you make real notes?
Use stickies? Use digital stickies? If you
primarily use "mental stickies," what kinds of
questions do you ask about what you read?

Write down some questions you might ask,
or notes you might make, about the texts
you have chosen.

2 Consider how you might use some terms from
Chapter 1 -- logos, ethos, pathos, and kairos --
to engage in active reading. Pick a
work you are reading for a class and make a
note of the following: the subject, how the text
builds logos, how the writer establishes ethos,
how the text demonstrates a use of pathos, and
how the writer shows an awareness of kairos.

What do you discover? How might attending to
these rhetorical dimensions improve your ability
to read -- and summarize -- a text?

3

Choose a text that you might be called upon to analyze, such as a journal article, a work of art, or a video or film. Make a list of all of the questions you have about it, as well as all of the points that you find interesting.

Next, make a list of quotations, still images, characteristics of the work, or other information that has popped out at you during your reading of the text.

Now group these pieces according to criteria that make sense to you, as Liz does with the images from Frederick Douglass's *Narrative* on pp. 87-89. Consider the questions you listed in light of your arrangement of pieces from the text. Rearrange questions and textual evidence as needed. What new insights emerge for you from this process?

4

Think about the book you're reading right now -- *Understanding Rhetoric*. Look back at the discussion on pp. 83-84 of Frederick Douglass's interest in controlling the way he appeared in images in print. Why do you think that this book uses Douglass as an example? What evidence do you find that indicates that the writers and illustrators of this book thought carefully about the images it includes? What choices might you have made differently?

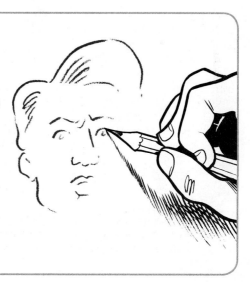

bedfordstmartins.com/understandingrhetoric

121

FOR EXAMPLE, FORMER COLLEGE PROFESSOR BARBARA EHRENREICH TOOK MINIMUM-WAGE JOBS TO RESEARCH HER BOOK *NICKEL AND DIMED*, ABOUT THE STRUGGLES OF THE WORKING POOR.

EHRENREICH TOLD HOW THINGS HAPPENED FROM HER OWN PERSPECTIVE.

SCRUB!!

SCRUB!

SCRUB!

RINSE!

WHEN SHE SAT DOWN TO COMPOSE HER ACTUAL TEXT, SHE WASN'T PRETENDING ANYMORE.

EXACTLY. ADOPTING AN IDENTITY CAN BE ABOUT DOING **REAL RESEARCH** -- NOT JUST PUTTING ON A COSTUME.

WHY ARE YOU -- ?

DON'T ASK.

WRITERS NEED TO BE CLEAR ABOUT WHY THEIR PERSPECTIVES ARE DISTINCTIVE AND USEFUL TO OTHERS.

LITTLE HELP?

AFTER ALL, WHO YOU ARE AS AN INDIVIDUAL IS ABOUT A LOT MORE THAN JUST ASSUMING A ONE-TIME ROLE.

129

131

137

As a founder of Gang of Geeks, a group of engineering students and actors devoted to making funny videos about surviving the first year as an engineering student, I've learned a lot about how to organize and plan an entertaining performance, give audiences a rewarding experience, and use social media creatively to promote our work. We've also involved local high school kids to encourage them to explore the creative aspects of math and engineering and to make college look like fun. As an intern in the Shakespeare Festival, I would bring fresh ideas about community outreach and a youthful sensibility to our productions, while also using my practical skills to help with inventory, accounting, and other offstage matters.

COMING UP IN THE NEXT EXCITING EPISODE OF REFRAME

"The OFFICE Hour!"

[pg. 171]

DRAWING CONCLUSIONS

The following assignments ask you to
think about creating effective arguments.

1 This chapter mentions Barbara Ehrenreich's *Nickel and Dimed*, a book about the struggles of the working poor that relies on the author's experience of getting by on minimum-wage jobs.

What personal experiences have you had that connect you to an idea or a subject that interests you? How can you use your experiences to explore that subject in a piece of writing? Draft a proposal for a writing project in a genre of your choosing (perhaps a Web essay or a newspaper editorial) that uses your firsthand experience to enhance the discussion of your topic.

2 Keep notes for a week about how you interact with others through various online sites. How do you represent yourself -- in filling out required or requested information, in uploading content, and in interacting with others?

Write a short autoethnography -- a brief narrative describing your own use of the sites -- that analyzes your experiences and discusses how you use different identities in different rhetorical situations.

Look at pp. 127-28 of this chapter, in which extreme and bland tones are represented both verbally and visually. Choose a short text, such as an email or online posting, that you have written in the past month with a particular audience in mind.

Who is the audience? What tone do you take in your writing? Turn your original text into an audience-appropriate media text (perhaps a comic, collage, poster, or video) that uses visuals or other nonverbal means to help convey tone.

Many students feel anxiety about public speaking and presenting their ideas in front of large groups of people. What is the largest audience that you have ever had to address? How did you prepare for your presentation?

Looking back, what worked well, and what should you have done differently? How did the composition of the audience affect how you felt about your performance?

bedfordstmartins.com/understandingrhetoric

Issue 4 • Argument Beyond Pro and Con

Issue 4 • Argument Beyond Pro and Con

Issue 4 • Argument Beyond Pro and Con

EMBEDDED IN ALL OF THOSE "QUESTION WORDS" IS A COMPLEX SET OF:

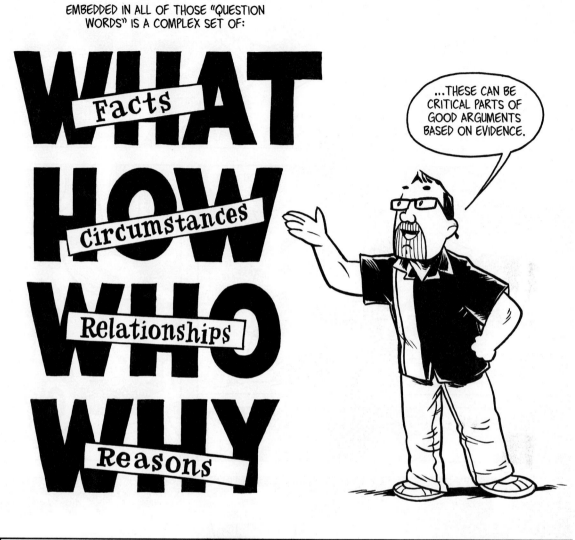

WHAT
Facts

HOW
Circumstances

WHO
Relationships

WHY
Reasons

...THESE CAN BE CRITICAL PARTS OF GOOD ARGUMENTS BASED ON EVIDENCE.

NOW -- WHAT IN THE **WORLD**?

POLICE

AHEM.

EVIDENCE CAN COME FROM COMPARING ONE CASE TO ANOTHER...

...AND FROM EXPERTS WHO CAN PROVIDE INFORMED **OPINIONS**.

THIS YOUNG WOMAN...

...WAS SUFFER- ING FROM **MALNOURISHMENT** AND **SLEEP DEPRIVATION**...

...THAT RENDERED HER INCAPABLE OF KNOWING RIGHT FROM WRONG.

ARGUMENTS IN COURT FOLLOW HIGHLY SPECIALIZED RULES...

...THAT DETERMINE WHAT EVIDENCE CAN BE INCLUDED, THE ORDER OF THE PRESENTATION...

BANG BANG

ORDER!

LIZ!

...AND EVEN WHICH INFORMATION THE AUDIENCE -- THE JURORS -- CAN CONSIDER.

BOOT!

159

The increasing generational differences between immigrants from Japan, the Issei, and the American-born second generation, the Nisei, had divided Japanese Americans even prior to the outbreak of World War II, and this division grew more apparent in the camps in which many Japanese Americans were interned during the war years. Nisei Gene Sogioka noted during his internment, "It's not just the age gap.... There are two different cultures in the camp: the Nisei, and the Issei"(qtd. in Gesenseway 153). The disparity between ancient Japan and modernized America was embodied and displayed by the contrasting values, ideologies, and lifestyles of the Issei and Nisei. The Issei often insisted that Japanese be spoken throughout the camp; the Nisei, however, symbolized the idealistic quest for the "American Dream" and willingly conformed to U.S. customs (Dusselier 195). The camp structure intensified the estrangement between Issei parents and their Nisei children because the young people were no longer economically dependent on their parents; by taking away any rights to income or social status, the U.S. government had usurped the position of primary caregiver, and the structure of the Japanese American family unit neared disintegration (Ziegler 136; Dusselier 194). Due to the inability of each group to understand or accept the other's behaviors, an antagonistic relationship developed. Ted Matsuda, interned at Jerome, Arkansas, describes in his evacuation diary the frequent problems with stealing occurring in the camp (21). In his June 15 entry, he bitterly recounts, "Issei are quick to blame every fault on the Nisei" (21). Through the disunion between the Issei and Nisei, the cultural identification term "Japanese American" became fragmented by the opposing sides of its two competing ethnicities.

Adapted from an essay by Marissa Osato

Issue 4 • Argument Beyond Pro and Con

IN FACT, THE LAWS CREATED BY THE FAMILY EDUCATIONAL RIGHTS AND PRIVACY ACT [FERPA] REQUIRE THAT STUDENTS WAIVE IN WRITING THEIR RIGHT TO PRIVACY IF THEY'D LIKE THEIR PARENTS TO KNOW ABOUT THEIR GRADES.

CINDY'S GRADES

SO THE **LAW** IS ACTUALLY ON THE SIDE OF STUDENTS' PRIVACY.

WE CAN ARGUE WHETHER THAT LAW IS GOOD OR NOT.

the LAW

IS IT USEFUL AND HELPFUL FOR STUDENTS' SUCCESS IN COLLEGE?

WE COULD ALSO ASK ABOUT **CAUSE AND EFFECT** -- HOW MIGHT THE FERPA GUIDELINES LEAD TO GREATER STUDENT RESPONSIBILITY?

CAUSE & EFFECT

OR **NOT**?

ARGUING ALONG THESE LINES MIGHT ALSO ALLOW US TO ADDRESS THE QUESTION OF THE VALUES REPRESENTED BY THE GUIDELINES.

VALUES

FURTHERMORE, WHILE WE SEEM TO BE STARTING FROM DIFFERENT POSITIONS IN THIS ARGUMENT...

...WE SHOULD ALSO CONSIDER WHAT BOTH POSITIONS HAVE IN COMMON.

YES!

BOTH ASSERTIONS ARE FRAMED BY THE DESIRE TO HAVE STUDENTS **SUCCEED** IN COLLEGE!

Issue 4 • Argument Beyond Pro and Con

169

AND THE LAST SENTENCE ACTUALLY WORKS AS A TRANSITION TO THE BEGINNING OF THE FOLLOWING PARAGRAPH.

HERE, THE TOPIC SENTENCE IS ACTUALLY THE **SECOND** SENTENCE IN THE PARAGRAPH.

YOU CAN TELL FROM KAMENETZ'S CHOICE OF WORDS THAT SHE IS GOING TO ARGUE WITH THE ADMINISTRATORS.

SHE CALLS THEIR DEFENSE A "PREFERRED EXCUSE" RATHER THAN AN ARGUMENT SUPPORTED BY THE FACTS!

...h buyers and ...ng information, prices are likely ...n care, for example, comparison ...xpertise ...the patients ...arious treatments. In ...ls of educa... too, sho... ...ous transp...cy. The scho... have ...s ve...le transp...cy. ...em everythi... about ...have ...lity to pay for the education, ...d ...out ...cost of supplying it. It's even worse than an airline, where people sitting in adjoining seats may have paid very different fares. "In higher ed everyone is paying a radically different price for the same good. . . . If you want to get suspicious about it, it's cartel behavior."

College administrators don't like being referred to as a cartel, a group that colludes to set prices. Their preferred excuse for raising tuition is their own operating costs, especially wages. . . .

WOW.

THERE'S A LOT GOING ON IN THIS BOOK!

I CAN DEFINITELY SEE HOW SHE'S BUILDING HER ARGUMENT.

SPEAKING OF ARGUMENTS... CAN WE TAKE A LOOK AT MY DRAFT NOW?

COMING UP IN THE NEXT EXCITING EPISODE OF **REFRAME**

"Get a CLUE!"

[pg. 207]

DRAWING CONCLUSIONS

The following assignments ask you to
think about creating effective arguments.

1 Map out the financial and personal costs of your
college education and the financial and personal
gains you hope to get from it. Use both text
and visuals to present compelling information
about your college costs.

What argument do you think your map
is making? Write a few paragraphs
explaining how you would persuade an
interested audience (such as a family
member) that your studies are -- or
are not -- worthwhile.

2 Think about the various ways in which students highlight and otherwise
graphically engage with their books. Pick a paragraph from an academic
or personal argument you have written recently. Mark up the material,
using highlighters of different colors, sticky notes, annotations, or other
methods, to identify topic sentences, supporting claims,
and data, along with any counterarguments.

What does such annotation tell you about how
you developed your argument? What might
you do differently to revise the work and, if
necessary, create a more balanced argument?

3

Proving causality often requires consideration of multiple factors and complex processes. Focus on some aspect of a contemporary issue (such as cyberbullying) that interests you and brainstorm with a partner about the various possible causes and effects. Can you suggest other potential causes of a given effect? What evidence might support the idea that an effect actually springs from a cause you identify?

Write or sketch out a chain of causes and effects leading to and from the issue on which you are focusing, and make notes on at least two points that will help you better understand or address the issue. What information would you need to convince classmates that your explanation of causes and effects makes sense? For instance, you might trace the various causes that have led people to believe that cyberbullying is a serious Internet issue -- while you also investigate the perspective of those who think the issue isn't a particularly serious problem.

4

Create a plan for a Web site that would discuss in an engaging way the issue you identified in assignment 3. How would you show the seriousness (or lack of seriousness) of the issue to a particular audience? What evidence would you need to include on the site, and how would you present that evidence -- using links? text? images? media files? How would you organize the site?

Present your plan to a small group of classmates and collect feedback on your site proposal.

bedfordstmartins.com/understandingrhetoric

Issue 5 • Research: More Than Detective Work

Issue 5 • Research: More Than Detective Work

Successful DETECTION & RESEARCH tips!

START

Distinguish between PRIMARY and SECONDARY sources

RESEARCH as widely as possible

READ as much of each SOURCE as possible

EVALUATE your sources

★ LOSE A TURN! ★

SUMMARIZE or PARAPHRASE your sources—in your OWN WORDS!

Select useful QUOTATIONS

★ ROLL AGAIN! ★

Exercise CAUTION when CUTTING and PASTING SOURCES

GO BACK TO START

Always CITE SOURCES

GO BACK 2 SPACES

A+

189

Issue 5 • Research: More Than Detective Work

SOMETIMES EVEN THE "FACTS" OF HISTORICAL CASES MAY BE OPEN TO DEBATE.

RAINFALL STATISTICS AND THE LOCATIONS OF PROPERTY LINES WEREN'T RECORDED AS CAREFULLY IN 1692 AS THEY ARE TODAY.

JOURNAL of ECONOMIC PERSPECTIVE

SOME SCHOLARS HAVE ARGUED THAT THE AFFLICTED PEOPLE OF SALEM WERE ACTUALLY HALLUCINATING AFTER EATING CONTAMINATED RYE.

RYE BREAD

YOU SHOULD CONSULT MULTIPLE SOURCES TO GET A SENSE OF THE SCHOLARLY DEBATES SURROUNDING YOUR RESEARCH TOPIC. NOT EVERYONE AGREES THAT WHAT THE PURITANS ATE WAS TO BLAME FOR THE SALEM WITCH HYSTERIA.

JOURNAL of RYE
R.Q. RYE QUARTERLY
STUDY: Rye Best for Grilled Cheese

CAST A WIDE NET FOR YOUR RESEARCH AND READ THROUGH ALL THE LIBRARY RECORDS OR SEARCH SCREENS. DON'T STOP AT THE FIRST PAGE OF RESULTS.

OF COURSE, IF YOU TURN UP THOUSANDS OF GOOGLE HITS, YOU NEED TO NARROW YOUR SEARCH, BEFORE YOU READ THROUGH THE RESULTS.

HMMM...

BIBLIOGRAPHY
Aaronson, Albert
Alabaster, Arthur
Amand, Alexandra
Anderson, Alice
April, Anders
Arlington, Alan
Atwood, Ambrose
That's it!

193

Jonathan Alexander says:
HOWEVER, THERE ARE SOME SITUATIONS WHERE ONLINE SOURCES WITH A STRONG SELF-INTEREST, SUCH AS TWEETS AND STATUS UPDATES, MAY GIVE AN INSIDER'S VIEW OF CURRENT EVENTS.

@Lizlosh
THINK ABOUT WHICH SOURCES WILL BEST SERVE YOUR PURPOSE IN THIS CONTEXT.

89/160 Remaining

YOU CAN ALSO LOOK FOR INFORMATION ABOUT THE CREATOR OF A POTENTIAL SOURCE.

IS THIS PERSON A SCHOLAR, AN EXPERT, OR AN INFORMED OBSERVER? HOW CAN YOU FIND OUT?

IF THE PERSON TEACHES AT A UNIVERSITY, YOU MIGHT LOOK AT HIS OR HER FACULTY WEB PAGE.

Alexander, Jonathan

Professor of English and Director of the Center for Excellence in Writing and Communication at the University of California, Irvine.

IT MIGHT GIVE YOU A BETTER SENSE OF THE SCHOLAR'S PERSONALITY, RESEARCH INTERESTS, AND DEPTH OF KNOWLEDGE ON THE SUBJECT.

MAKING SOURCES TALK: SUMMARY, PARAPHRASE, QUOTATION

SUMMARY

SETTING UP CONTEXTS AND PROVIDING BACKGROUND INFORMATION

PARAPHRASE

GIVING A SENSE OF THE AUTHOR'S ARGUMENT

QUOTATION

DRAWING ATTENTION TO SOMETHING PARTICULARLY EVOCATIVE OR INSIGHTFUL IN THE AUTHOR'S OWN WORDS

LET'S TALK ABOUT SUMMARIZING, PARAPHRASING, AND QUOTING -- HOW TO DO THEM, WHEN, AND WHY.

SUMMARIZING

PRESENTS A CONCISE, GENERAL SENSE OF WHAT YOUR SOURCE IS ABOUT.

OFTEN, SUMMARIZING GIVES A BROAD OVERVIEW OF MATERIAL THAT IS NOT IN DISPUTE.

HERE'S A SUMMARY THAT USES CONTENT FROM A WIKIPEDIA ARTICLE:

"The history of detective fiction dates back to 1841, when Edgar Allan Poe introduced Monsieur C. Auguste Dupin in the short story 'The Murders in the Rue Morgue.' Today it includes the police procedural, the legal thriller, the courtroom drama, the locked room mystery, hard-boiled fiction, the noir novel, and the 'cozy,' in which sex and violence are downplayed. In the 'cozy,' the protagonist is often a female amateur, and humor and social satire might be important parts of the narrative."

WIKIPEDIA

PARAPHRASING SHOULD GIVE THE READER A MORE COMPLETE SENSE OF THE AUTHOR'S ARGUMENT AND MORE OF THE FLAVOR OF THE ORIGINAL THAN A SUMMARY.

AND EVEN THOUGH A PARAPHRASE IS "IN YOUR OWN WORDS," THE IDEAS CAME FROM SOMEWHERE ELSE -- SO YOU'LL HAVE TO CITE YOUR SOURCE.

HERE'S A PARAPHRASE OF PART OF A CHAPTER IN THE BOOK *CITY OF QUARTZ*, A HISTORY OF LOS ANGELES.

AUTHOR MIKE DAVIS CLAIMS THAT NOIR STORIES ABOUT CRIME AND THE ILL EFFECTS OF CAPITALISM REFLECT MANY DIFFERENT INFLU-ENCES FROM THE TIME OF THE GREAT DEPRESSION, WORLD WAR II, AND THE PERIOD THAT FOLLOWED.

DAVIS ARGUES THAT IMMIGRANT WRITERS, COMPOSERS, FILMMAKERS, AND ARTISTS FLEEING HITLER'S GERMANY PLAYED A ROLE IN DEVELOPING CERTAIN ASPECTS OF THE NOIR DETECTIVE GENRE, BUT HE INSISTS THAT FEW OF THEM ACTUALLY PARTICIPATED IN THE GRITTY URBAN LIFESTYLES OF LOS ANGELES IN THE 1940s.

UNLIKE MANY CRITICS, DAVIS ASSERTS THAT LOCAL LOS ANGELES AUTHORS PLAYED A MAJOR ROLE IN DEVELOP-ING WHAT CAME TO BE KNOWN AS "L.A. NOIR."

HE SAYS THAT THESE LOCAL WRITERS KNEW MUCH MORE ABOUT THE SCANDALS OF THE CITY -- POLICE CORRUPTION, REAL ESTATE AND OIL SPECULATION, AND ANTI-LABOR AND ANTI-IMMIGRANT POLITICS -- THAN OUTSIDERS COMING FROM EUROPE DID.

Issue 5 • Research: More Than Detective Work

Issue 5 • Research: More Than Detective Work

☐ 1. <u>Genetic Models of Homosexuality: Generating Testable Predictions</u> 🔍

<u>Sergey Gavrilets</u>, <u>William R. Rice</u>
Proceedings: Biological Sciences, Vol. 273, No. 1605 (Dec. 22, 2006), pp. 3031-3038
<u>Page Scan</u> <u>Article PDF</u> <u>Article Summary</u>

☐ 2. <u>Aquinas on Natural Law and the Virtues in Biblical Context:</u>
<u>Homosexuality as a Test Case</u> 🔍

<u>Eugene F. Rogers Jr.</u>
The Journal of Religious Ethics, Vol. 27, No. 1 (Spring, 1999), pp. 29-56
<u>Page Scan</u> <u>Article PDF</u> <u>Article Summary</u>

☐ 3. <u>Beliefs about the Origins of Homosexuality and Support for Gay Rights:</u>
<u>An Empirical Test of Attribution Theory</u>
<u>Donald P. Haider-Markel</u>, <u>Mark R. Joslyn</u>
The Public Opinion Quarterly, Vol. 72, No. 2 (Summer, 2008), pp. 291-310

☐ 4. <u>Scientif[...] [an]alyses of Homosexuality: A[...]</u>
[...]Method[...]

<u>Stephen J[...]</u>
The Journal of Religious Ethics, Vol. 25, No. 1 (Spring, 1997), pp. 89[...]
<u>Page Scan</u> <u>Article PDF</u> <u>Article Summary</u>

☐ 5. <u>Attributions and the Regulation of Marriage: Considering the Parallels</u>
<u>between Race and Homosexuality</u> 🔍

<u>Donald P. Haider-Markel</u>, <u>Mark R. Joslyn</u>
PS: Political Science and Politics, Vol. 38, No. 2 (Apr., 2005), pp. 233-239
<u>Page Scan</u> <u>Article PDF</u> <u>Article Summary</u>

☐ 6. <u>Male Homosexuality: Absence of Linkage to Microsatellite Markers at</u>
<u>Xq28</u> 🔍

<u>George Rice</u>, <u>Carol Anderson</u>, <u>Neil Risch</u>, <u>George Ebers</u>
Science, New Series, Vol. 284, No. 5414 (Apr. 23, 1999), pp. 665-66[...]
<u>Page Scan</u> <u>Article PDF</u> <u>Article Summary</u>

7. **Origins Of Homosexuality** 🔍

John D. Rainer, G. Hav
The British Medical Journal, Vol. 2, No. 5476 (Dec. 18, 1965), p. 1488
Page Scan   Article PDF   Article Summary

8. **The Origins of Anthropological Genetics** FREE 🔍

Jonathan Marks
Current Anthropology, Vol. 53, No. S5, The Biological Anthropology of Living Human Populations: World Histories, National Styles, and International Networks (April 2012), pp. S161-S172
Full Text   Article PDF   Article Summary

HOW FAR BACK SHOULD RESEARCH GO?

9. **Do Biological Explanations of Homosexuality Have Moral, Legal, or Policy Implications?** 🔍

Aaron S. Greenberg, J. Michael Bailey
The Journal of Sex Research, Vol. 30, No. 3 (Aug., 1993), pp. 245-251
Page Scan   Article PDF   Article Summary

10. **Evidence for Homosexuality Gene** 🔍

Robert Pool
Science, New Series, Vol. 261, No. 5119 (Jul. 16, 1993), pp. 291-2
Page Scan   Article PDF   Article Summary

SCIENCE IS A TOP PEER-REVIEWED SCIENCE JOURNAL.

11. **Biological Determinism and Homosexuality** 🔍

Bonnie Spanier
NWSA Journal, Vol. 7, No. 1, Sexual Orientation (Spring, 1995), pp. 54-71
Page Scan   Article PDF   Article Summary

Sex-Peptide Is the Molecular ... *Drosophila melanogaster* 🔍

Hua-fa Liu, Eric Kubli
Proceedings of the National Academy of Sciences of the United States of America, Vol. 100, No. 17 (Aug. 19, 2003), pp. 9929-9933
Page Scan   Article PDF   Article Summary

THE NATIONAL WOMEN'S STUDIES ASSOCIATION JOURNAL MIGHT OFFER A FEMINIST INTERPRETATION.

DRAWING CONCLUSIONS

The following assignments ask you to practice finding,
evaluating, and responding to research sources.

1 Choose a historical event that interests
you. Conduct an Internet search to get
an overview of the kinds of sources on
that subject that you can find outside the
library. (Keep track of the search terms
you use, and make a note of those that seem
to produce the most effective results.)

Bookmark the information that seems most
current, most reliable, and most intriguing. What
makes you trust or distrust the sources you find?

2 Create a research log to follow up on the event you
investigated in assignment 1. Collect and organize the
citation information about each Internet source that you
consider or even look at briefly. Now go to the library
and discuss the information you've gathered so far with a
research librarian.

What other kinds of sources does the library offer --
database articles, special collections -- that you can't find
online? Find at least five library sources that may be useful
for your project and record bibliographic information and a
brief summary of each. (If you like, you can use a camera or
phone to record visual and audio notes about books, images,
and people relevant to your project.)

3

Find at least two primary sources with first-person accounts of the historical event you began investigating in assignment 1. (Remember that illustrations and other images can be primary sources, too.)

Lay out a storyboard that illustrates those accounts of the event and shows how they relate to each other. Do they depict the event from similar perspectives? Do they differ in significant ways? Create a brief explanation of the questions that you uncover in examining these different accounts.

4

A good way to begin creating a research-based argument is to find a position that you will refute or critique. Think about your position on some significant aspect of the event you have begun researching. (In this chapter, for instance, Jonathan and Liz explore different explanations for the witchcraft hysteria around Salem Village.)

Find a source -- perhaps one that is already part of the research log you began in assignment 2 -- that takes a thoughtful position that differs from your own. Summarize that source's argument fairly, and then sketch out a chart or an outline of your response.

bedfordstmartins.com/understandingrhetoric

219

THE FIRST VERSION OF AUSTEN'S HAPPY ENDING COMES ABOUT BECAUSE THE HEROINE IS TRICKED INTO BEING ALONE WITH THE HERO. WHEN HE DECLARES HIS LOVE FOR HER IN VERY CONVENTIONAL LANGUAGE, SHE DOESN'T HAVE MUCH TO SAY IN RESPONSE.

BECAUSE AUSTEN WASN'T HAPPY WITH THE ENDING OF HER NOVEL, SHE REVISED RADICALLY.

SHE CREATED A BRAND-NEW SCENE IN WHICH A LOT WAS GOING ON BECAUSE THE CHARACTERS IN THE STORY WERE PREPARING FOR A WEDDING.

Mrs. Musgrove giving Mrs. Croft the history of her eldest daughter's engagement.

Mary and Henrietta heading out the front door for a walk.

Captain Wentworth secretly writing a love letter to Anne.

Captain Harville and Anne arguing about whether men or women are more faithful.

Persuasion

IN THE REVISED ENDING, AUSTEN'S HEROINE SHOWS HERSELF TO BE A SOPHISTICATED CONVERSATIONALIST IN A DEBATE ABOUT WHETHER MEN OR WOMEN ARE MORE FAITHFUL IN LOVE.

ALTHOUGH HE DOESN'T SEEM TO BE PAYING ATTENTION, THE DASHING HERO IS ACTUALLY LISTENING TO HER ARGUMENT ATTENTIVELY.

WHILE ALL THE ACTION IS GOING ON AROUND HIM, HE WRITES HER A LETTER TO TELL HER HOW HE REALLY FEELS.

I DEFINITELY LIKE THAT ENDING BETTER.

IT IS A LOT MORE RHETORICALLY INTERESTING.

OF COURSE, A MORE ELABORATE SOLUTION TO A PROBLEM IN A PIECE OF WRITING ISN'T ALWAYS THE RIGHT APPROACH.

SOMETIMES A SIMPLER SOLUTION IS BETTER.

TEMPUS FUGIT

BUT WHETHER YOU'RE REVISING A NOVEL OR A PIECE OF ACADEMIC WRITING...

...IT'S IMPORTANT TO GIVE YOURSELF ENOUGH TIME TO MAKE MAJOR REVISIONS, AS AUSTEN DID.

SEWARD WAS RIGHT TO BE WORRIED. LINCOLN'S EARLY DRAFTS FOR THE INAUGURAL ADDRESS WERE EXTREMELY CONFRONTATIONAL.

In your hands, my dissatisfied fellow countrymen, and not in mine, is the momentous issue of civil war. The government will not assail you, unless you first assail it. You can have no conflict, without being yourselves the aggressors. You have no oath registered in Heaven to destroy the government, while I shall have the most solemn one to "preserve, protect, and defend" it. You can forbear the assault upon it; I can not shrink from the defense of it. With you, and not with me, is the solemn question of "Shall it be peace, or a sword?"

HE'S PRACTICALLY DARING SLAVEHOLDING STATES TO REVOLT.

"SHALL IT BE PEACE, OR A SWORD?" WHAT A TERRIBLE ENDING!

WHAT IS HE **THINKING**?

SEWARD LATER EXPLAINED WHAT HE SAW AS THE FLAW IN LINCOLN'S ORIGINAL APPROACH:

...we must CHANGE THE QUESTION BEFORE THE PUBLIC FROM ONE UPON SLAVERY, OR ABOUT SLAVERY, for a question upon UNION OR DISUNION.

SEWARD KNEW THAT THE FINAL WORDS OF THE SPEECH WERE GOING TO HAVE THE MOST RHETORICAL IMPACT. SO HE OFFERED THE PRESIDENT SOME DIFFERENT OPTIONS FOR WORDING AND SUGGESTED TWO DIFFERENT ENDINGS.

LIKE ANY GOOD PEER REVIEWER, SEWARD GAVE HIS PARTNER SOME CHOICES.

LINCOLN LIKED THE SECOND OF SEWARD'S SUGGESTED CLOSING PARAGRAPHS BETTER.

The mystic chords which proceeding from so many battle fields and so many patriot graves pass through all the hearts and all the hearths in this broad continent of ours will yet again harmonize in their ancient music when breathed upon by the guardian angel of the nation.

LINCOLN APPROVED OF SEWARD'S COMPLEX METAPHOR OF A MUSICAL STRING CONNECTING TWO POINTS.

THIS RHETORICAL FIGURE REPRESENTED THE EMOTIONAL BOND CONNECTING THE GRAVES OF REVOLUTIONARY SOLDIERS TO THE PEOPLE OF LINCOLN'S OWN DAY.

We are not enemies, but friends. We must not be enemies.

Though passion may have strained, it must not break our bonds of affection.

The mystic chords of memory, stretching from every battlefield, and patriot grave, to every living heart and hearthstone, all over this broad land, will yet swell the chorus of the Union, when again touched, as surely they will be, by the better angels of our nature.

WHEN YOUR OWN WORK IS REVIEWED BY OTHER PEOPLE, IT CAN BE IMPORTANT TO EVALUATE THEIR SUGGESTIONS.

ACCEPTING ALL ADVICE FROM OTHERS UNCRITICALLY CAN BE ALMOST AS BAD AS REFUSING TO LISTEN TO FEEDBACK IN THE FIRST PLACE.

BE AN ACTIVE PARTICIPANT IN YOUR REVISION PROCESS AT EVERY STAGE OF DRAFTING.

233

*For more on research, see CHAPTER 5.

"Since the dawn of time, art has made the expression of ideas and feelings possible.

This makes art a hugely important part of all human life.

Art even appears in caves that were visited by ancient humans, and art remains an important part of basically every culture everywhere around the globe . . ."

COMING UP IN THE NEXT EXCITING EPISODE OF **REFRAME**

"How does this LOOK?"

[pg. 267]

DRAWING CONCLUSIONS

The following assignments ask you to
think about your revision process.

1 Getting suggestions for improving your writing can be painful, even when your reviewer's intentions are good. Think about the kinds of feedback that you find most helpful and the ways you prefer to hear from peer reviewers (changes tracked in a document? verbal comments? a letter from the reviewer?). Compose an email to your peer review group outlining the kinds of feedback you prefer and the manner in which you want to receive that feedback.

If your class doesn't use peer review groups, consider starting one of your own. Most successful writers use them all the time!

2 Think about the last time you were in an argument -- and lost. With whom were you arguing? What was the argument about? If you could go back and change how you approached the argument, what would you do differently? Would you try a different rhetorical approach? Would you use different evidence to support your claims? Would you modify your primary claims to achieve a different outcome, such as a compromise?

Compose a short essay in which you describe the disagreement and analyze what was ineffective about your strategy and how you would modify it if you could replay the argument.

3

One fun strategy for "re-visioning" your work is to print out your writing assignment and then physically cut the paper into pieces. Cut out each paragraph, but also consider cutting individual paragraphs into two or more pieces. After jumbling up all the pieces, invite a reader to piece your work together again. You might find that another reader puts your work back together in interesting new ways.

Have introductory and concluding paragraphs changed places? Have body paragraphs moved around? Have paragraphs been rearranged? Reflect on whether the reorganization improves aspects of your writing. What changes do you want to keep?

4

Play "search and destroy" using the Find and Replace commands in your word processing program. If you notice (or a reviewer points out) that you rely too much on certain words or expressions, Find and Replace All of them with a word such as *BOOM!* You can then easily see where the overused material is so that you can change or delete it.

You can try a similar exercise if you discover that you use key terms or phrases too often in a single piece of writing. Use the Find command, but don't simply replace each word with a synonym; instead, consider how you can recast the sentence to avoid repeating the words.

bedfordstmartins.com/understandingrhetoric

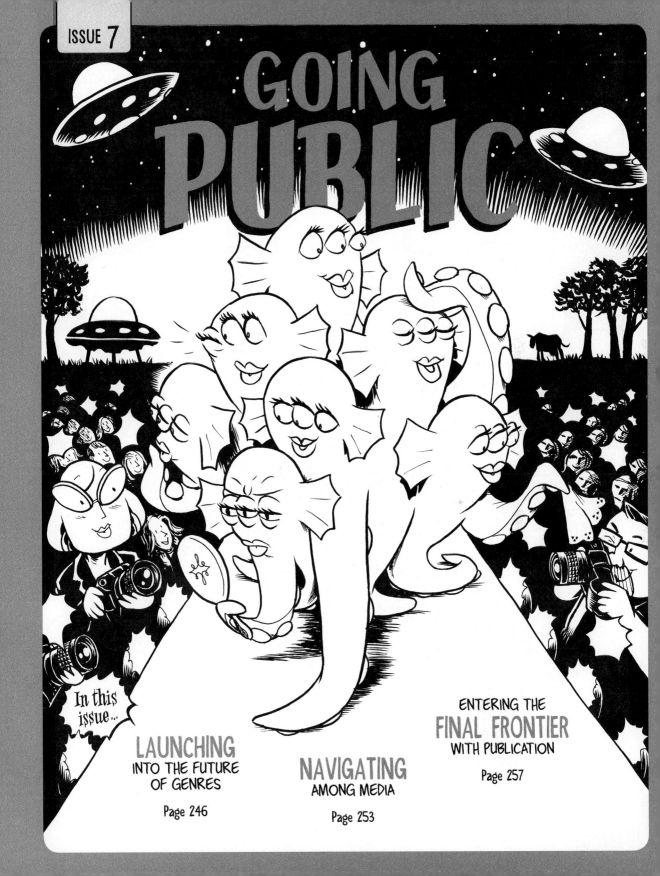

251

THE MOST INTERESTING AND ARTISTICALLY DECORATED CARDS GET POSTED ON THE POSTSECRET BLOG.

NOW THE IMAGES CAN BE SHARED...

Eating Broccoli makes me feel less sad.

Click to Enlarge

...AND COMMENTED UPON...

Love it!

LAME

nice! ;)

...BY OTHERS.

AFTER A FEW YEARS, MODERATOR FRANK WARREN CREATED A BOOK.

I'M REALLY QUITE MOROSE.

SO POSTSECRET HAS TRANSFORMED THE GENRE OF THE POSTCARD.

IT'S CHANGED EXPECTATIONS ABOUT WHAT MIGHT BE ON A POSTCARD: NOT NEWS ABOUT A VACATION, BUT **SECRETS**...

WEB-ISODES

SPEAKING TOUR

MOVIE

BLOG

SEQUEL

BOOKS

BOOP!

PODCAST

NOTES

AND IT'S CHANGED THE CONVENTIONS OF THE MEDIA AS WELL -- THE POSTCARDS ARE PART OF A BLOG, A BOOK, AND EVEN A SPEAKING TOUR.

GENERIC CONTENT

Issue 7 • Going Public

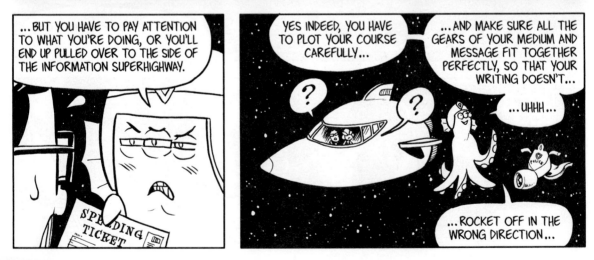

bits
Ideas for Teaching Composition

Home   About   RSS

Taking Comics Seriously

Elizabeth Losh, Director of Academic Programs at Sixth College of the University of California, San Diego, and Jonathan Alexander, Professor of English and the Campus Writing Coordinator at the University of California, Irvine, are collaborating with artists Zander Cannon and Kevin Cannon of Big Time Attic on Understanding Rhetoric: A Graphic Guide to Writing, a forthcoming comic-style text for first-year composition students.

Learning to See Writing
posted: 2.13.12 by Elizabeth Losh and Jonathan Alexander

Jonathan

[...]'s post about co-authoring *Understanding [R]hetoric: A Graphic Guide to Writing* mentions some [...]he challenges of working on a graphic book. For [...] one of the biggest challenges has been adapting [...] thinking and composing in a different medium. [In]deed, one of the lessons we have learned in the [pro]cess is that we can't just think like "text" [a]uthors; we also have to begin to think visually. As [w]e sketch out the chapters, panel by panel, we try to provide detailed visual cues for Kevin Cannon and Zander Cannon, our fabulous artists—who, in turn, not only modify our initial image directions and augment them beautifully, but have also challenged how we understand and use text in the graphic book form. (We'll be talking more about this process in our upcoming blogs.)

Along th[...], one of the earliest lessons we learned about our use of [...] we were initially relying too much on captioning and not [...] dialogue to carry the instructional weight of each chapter. That [...] were thinking like the text-producing scholars that we are, and not [...]he collaborative graphic authors we needed to be. We were constantly [ex]plaining rhetorical concepts, for instance, while ignoring how images and [di]alogue—the principal features of the comic form—could be used to [con]vey our ideas about writing. Comparing initial drafts of the first several [cha]pters with their more recent revisions shows a steady move away from [...]tioning to significantly more reliance on dialogue and visuals.

[Co]ncomitant with that shift has been a shift in how we think about the [pr]oject and the processes we have to engage in to maximize our use of the

Blogs

Search [...]

Recent [...]
> Manga [...]

DRAWING CONCLUSIONS

The following assignments ask you to think
about making your work available to audiences.

1 Moving your writing from one genre or medium to another
can be a powerful way to reexamine what you've
composed. Write or sketch a brief proposal to turn
an academic writing assignment into some other kind
of text, such as a brochure or an advertisement. What
choices help you communicate your primary ideas?

Reflect on what this "re-mediation" tells you about
what you chose to highlight. Are you making the same
main point (and making the main point equally clearly) in
both texts? Why or why not? What does your re-mediation
reveal about the academic assignment?

2 Reflect on your work by imagining how you might communicate your
ideas to different audiences or for different purposes. Take a piece you
have composed for an academic assignment and recast it for a different
audience. For instance, you might rewrite an analysis of a painting or
a lab report so that your parents or a younger sibling know what you're
talking about.

Reflect on how this
rewriting process
makes you rethink
your original piece
of writing.

3

Starting from the idea of a planet ruled by a cat, create works in at least two genres, choosing from these options or creating your own:

1) a one-page newspaper ad for a movie

2) a video trailer for a movie

3) a "short-short" or "flash fiction" story

4) a chapter of a comic book

5) an abstract for a scientific paper describing the imaginary planet

4

Make the work of assignment 3 public by posting a digital copy of it online. Send a link to your instructor along with a cover letter explaining your process of composition and reflecting on what you learned.

Did you collaborate with others in creating your content? Did you seek feedback on drafts? How closely did your method adhere to the approach outlined in this book? What parts of your process worked well, and what will you do differently the next time you tackle a similar project?

bedfordstmartins.com/understandingrhetoric

Acknowledgments

p. 16: *Casablanca* movie poster and still: Warner Brothers/Photofest.

p. 19: Human Rights Campaign logo: Courtesy of Human Rights Campaign.

p. 83: The New-York Historical Society. Frederick Douglass portrait. File PR-052.

pp. 103–09: Jacket design by Susan Mitchell, and pages from the *9/11 Report: A Graphic Adaptation* by Sid Jacobson and Ernie Colon. Copyright 2006 by Castlebridge Enterprises Inc. Reprinted by permission of Hill & Wang, a division of Farrar, Straus and Giroux.

p. 104: Cover of *9/11 Report:* Courtesy of W. W. Norton and Company.

pp. 173–74: Cover of Anya Kamenetz's *DIY U* © 2010 Chelsea Green Publishing, used with permission.

pp. 191, 193: Bettmann/Corbis.

pp. 209–13: Courtesy of JSTOR.

p. 268: Refugee Studies Centre/Oxford Department of International Studies.

GLOSSARY

INDEX

GLOSSARY

Analysis
A close examination of the parts of a text with the goal of interpreting it as a whole.

Argument
The primary purpose of a text, or the main claim it makes.

Assertion
A debatable claim.

Audience
The intended or accidental recipients of a communication.

Cause and effect
Tracing the reasons that led to an outcome, or anticipating the likely result of an event or circumstance.

Citation
The way the original source of a quotation, summary, or paraphrase is documented.

Comparison and contrast
Noting similarities and differences between two texts.

Composition
Creating a text in one or more media.

Conclusion
The end of a text that ties together its argument.

Context
The situation in which a text is created, including its creator, audience, purpose, medium, and genre, as well as other factors.

Credibility
The characteristic that makes a text believable.

Critical lens
A perspective or theoretical approach that provides a context for analysis.

Critical reading
An analytical approach to a text.

Discourse
Written or spoken communication, often characterized by its use in particular communities.

Ethos

The credibility or authority that a speaker or writer brings to a subject.

Evidence

The information used to support an argument.

Explication

Revealing or uncovering ideas that are not directly stated in a text.

Genre

A conventional format for presenting information and ideas.

Implicit messages

Ideas that are present in a text but not directly stated.

Integration

Weaving material from others' work into one's own text and adding commentary that explains the material's purpose and importance.

Interpretation

Using context and critical analysis to explain the meaning of a text.

Invention

Any technique (such as freewriting or brainstorming) for exploring new thoughts and ideas during the writing process.

Kairos

Awareness of the appropriate timing, occasion, or opportunity for a given rhetorical act.

Logos

Appeals to reason and logic in a text.

Medium (*plural,* Media)

Material that records, displays, stores, or spreads information.

Paraphrase

A detailed explanation of the contents of a source that rephrases the language of the original source.

Pathos

Appeals to emotion.

Peer revision *or* Peer review

The process of seeking feedback on a text from a classmate, colleague, or friend.

Glossary

Plagiarism
Presenting the work of another as one's own, whether accidentally or deliberately.

Primary source
A work that presents a firsthand account of an event or a time.

Purpose
The aim of a communication.

Quotation
Direct repetition of material from a source.

Reflection
In writing, an analysis of a completed project that considers what the writer learned during the writing process.

Remediation
Revising a text that appeared originally in one medium so that it is effective in another medium.

Revision
The process of rewriting to improve a text, often by viewing it from different perspectives.

Rhetoric
The practice or study of effective communication.

Rhetorical analysis
Examining how, what, and why a given text communicates.

Secondary source
A work that describes, analyzes, or interprets a firsthand account or original work.

Summary
A brief, general restatement of the content of a source.

Surface errors
Distracting mistakes in grammar, punctuation, or spelling.

Synthesis
Putting information from multiple sources together to make one unified meaning.

Text
In rhetorical terms, any communication in any medium—including print books, films, Web content, slide presentations, Facebook posts, and so on.

Thesis

The main idea that a text develops.

Tone

The attitude that a text conveys to an audience.

Visual literacy

The ability to analyze elements of a visual text.

Voice

In writing, the way a writer expresses the person behind the words.

Writing process

The steps writers take in composing a text, which can vary greatly from writer to writer and from situation to situation.

INDEX

Index

Index